MW01705287

Essential Insights from the spiritual teachings of Bahá'u'lláh and 'Abdu'l-Bahá

Truthfulness

Compiled and designed by Corinne Randall

To Masoud Yazdani, whose vision inspired the creation of these books, you will always be in our hearts.

First and foremost among the favours, which the Almighty hath conferred upon man, is the gift of understanding...

This gift giveth man the power to discern the truth in all things, leadeth him to that which is right, and helpeth him to discover the secrets of creation.

Bahá'u'lláh

O SON OF SPIRIT!

The best beloved of all things in My sight is Justice; turn not away therefrom if thou desirest Me, and neglect it not that I may confide in thee.

By its aid thou shalt see with thine own eyes and not through the eyes of others, and shalt know of thine own knowledge and not through the knowledge of thy neighbour.

Bahá'u'lláh

The essence of all that
We have revealed for
thee is Justice,

is for man to free himself
from idle fancy and imitation,
discern with the eye of oneness
His glorious handiwork,
and look into all things
with a searching eye.

Bahá'u'lláh

The Purpose of the one true God, exalted be His glory, in revealing Himself unto men is to lay bare those gems that lie hidden within the mine of their true and inmost selves.

Happy is the man that hath clung unto the truth, detached from all that is in the heavens and all that is on earth!

Bahá'u'lláh

In the kingdoms of earth and heaven there must needs be manifested a Being, an Essence Who shall act as a Manifestation and Vehicle for the transmission of the grace of the Divinity Itself, the Sovereign Lord of all.

Through the Teachings of this Day Star of Truth every man will advance and develop until he attaineth the station at which he can manifest all the potential forces with which his inmost true self hath been endowed.

Bahá'u'lláh

O My servants! Could ye apprehend with what wonders of My munificence and bounty I have willed to entrust your souls, ye would, of a truth, rid yourselves of attachment to all created things, and would gain a true knowledge of your own selves—a knowledge which is the same as the comprehension of Mine own Being.

Ye would find yourselves
independent of all else but Me,
and would perceive, with your
inner and outer eye, and as
manifest as the revelation of
My effulgent Name, the seas of
My loving-kindness and bounty
moving within you.

Bahá'u'lláh

This most great, this
fathomless and surging ocean
is near, astonishingly near,
unto you. Behold it is closer
to you than your life-vein!

Ye are better known to the inmates of the Kingdom on high than ye are known to your own selves.

Bahá'u'lláh

Truth may be likened to the sun!

The sun is the luminous body that disperses all shadows; in the same way does truth scatter the shadows of our imagination. As the sun gives life to the body of humanity so does truth give life to their souls.

Truth is a sun that rises from different points on the horizon. Sometimes the sun rises from the centre of the horizon, then in summer it rises farther north, in winter farther south—but it is always the self-same sun, however different are the points of its rising.

'Abdu'l-Bahá

Truth is one in all religions,
and by means of it
the unity of the world
can be realized.

All are seeking truth, and there are many roads leading thereto. Truth has many aspects, but it remains always and forever one...

The fact that we imagine ourselves to be right and everybody else wrong is the greatest of all obstacles in the path towards unity, and unity is necessary if we would reach truth, for truth is one.

'Abdu'l-Bahá

Truthfulness is the goodliest of qualities as it comprehendeth all other virtues.

Let your eye be chaste,
your hand faithful,
your tongue truthful
and your heart enlightened.

'Abdu'l-Bahá

Without truthfulness progress and success in all of the worlds of God are impossible for a soul. When this holy attribute is established in man, all the divine qualities will also become realized.

Truthfulness is the foundation of all the virtues of the world of humanity.

'Abdu'l-Bahá

"There was once a disciple of Muhammad who asked of another disciple, 'What shall I do to please God?' And the other disciple replied: 'Do not kill. Do not steal. Do not covet,' etc., etc., etc. A great many 'do nots'," the Master laughed. "He asked still another, 'What shall I do to become nearer to God?' And this one said: 'You must supplicate and pray. You must be generous. You must be courageous,' etc., etc., etc.

Then the disciple went to 'Ali. 'What do you say I should do in order to please God and to become nearer to Him?' 'One thing only: be truthful.' For," continued the Master, "if you are truthful, you cannot commit murder. You would have to confess it! Neither can you steal. You would have to confess it. So, if one is truthful, he possesses all the virtues".

Story told by 'Abdu'l-Bahá

We will now mention unto thee Trustworthiness and the station thereof in the estimation of God, thy Lord, the Lord of the Mighty Throne. One day of days We repaired unto Our Green Island. Upon Our arrival, We beheld its streams flowing, and its trees luxuriant, and the sunlight playing in their midst. Turning Our face to the right, We beheld what the pen is powerless to describe; nor can it set forth that which the eye of the Lord of Mankind witnessed in that most sanctified, that most sublime, that blest, and most exalted Spot. Turning, then, to the left We gazed on one of the Beauties of the Most Sublime Paradise, standing on a pillar of light, and calling aloud saying: 'O inmates of earth and heaven! Behold ye My beauty, and My radiance, and My revelation, and My effulgence. By God, the True One! I am Trustworthiness and the revelation thereof, and the beauty thereof. I will recompense whosoever will cleave unto Me, and recognize My rank and station, and hold fast unto My hem. I am the most great ornament of the people of Bahá, and the vesture of glory unto all who are in the kingdom of creation. I am the supreme instrument for the prosperity of the world, and the horizon of assurance unto all beings.'

Bahá'u'lláh

Trustworthiness is the greatest portal leading unto the tranquillity and security of the people. In truth the stability of every affair hath depended and doth depend upon it. All the domains of power, of grandeur and of wealth are illumined by its light.

Beautify your tongues,
O people, with truthfulness,
and adorn your souls with
the ornament of honesty.

Bahá'u'lláh

Let truthfulness and courtesy be your adorning.

*Suffer not yourselves to
be deprived of the robe
of forbearance and justice,
that the sweet savours of
holiness may be wafted
from your hearts upon all
created things.*

Bahá'u'lláh

The worst human quality
and the most great sin
is backbiting.

A kindly tongue is the lodestone of the hearts of men. It is the bread of the spirit, it clotheth the words with meaning, it is the fountain of the light of wisdom and understanding...

'Abdu'l-Bahá

You must not see evil as evil and then compromise with your opinion, for to treat in a smooth, kindly way one whom you consider evil or an enemy is hypocrisy, and this is not worthy or allowable.

You must consider your enemies as your friends, look upon your evil-wishers as your well-wishers and treat them accordingly.

'Abdu'l-Bahá

Let not your heart be offended with anyone...

Turn all your thoughts toward bringing joy to hearts.

To look always at the good
and not at the bad.

If a man has ten good qualities
and one bad one, to look at the ten
and forget the one;

and if a man has ten bad qualities
and one good one, to look at the one
and forget the ten.

'Abdu'l-Bahá

The members of a Spiritual Assembly must take counsel together in such wise that no occasion for ill-feeling or discord may arise. This can be attained when every member expresseth with absolute freedom his own opinion and setteth forth his argument.

Should anyone oppose, he must on no account feel hurt for not until matters are fully discussed can the right way be revealed. The shining spark of truth cometh forth only after the clash of differing opinions.

'Abdu'l-Bahá

It were better for thee that
thou shouldst be a blasphemer
and tell the truth
than that thou shouldst
mouth the formulas of faith
and yet be a liar.

'Abdu'l-Bahá

Be thou of the people of hell-fire,
but be not a hypocrite.

Be thou an unbeliever, but be not a plotter.

Make thy home in taverns,
but tread not the path of the mischief-maker.

Fear thou God, but not the priest.

Give to the executioner thy head,
but not thy heart.

Let thine abode be under the stone,
but seek not the shelter of the cleric.

Bahá'u'lláh

*Fair speech and truthfulness,
by reason of their lofty rank
and position, are regarded
as a sun shining above
the horizon of knowledge.*

The waves rising from this Ocean are apparent before the eyes of the peoples of the world and the effusions of the Pen of wisdom and utterance are manifest everywhere.

Bahá'u'lláh

All those who seek truth
in the Heavenly Kingdom
shine like stars; they are
like fruit trees laden with
choice fruit, like seas full
of precious pearls.

'Abdu'l-Bahá

Peace be upon him whom the light of truth guideth unto all truth, and who, in the name of God, standeth in the path of His Cause, upon the shore of true understanding.

Bahá'u'lláh

REFERENCES

pp. 2-3. Bahá'u'lláh, *Gleanings from the Writings of Bahá'u'lláh,* US Baha'i Publishing Trust, 1990 pocket-size edition, XCV: p.198

pp. 4-5. Bahá'u'lláh, *The Hidden Words,* no. 2 from the Arabic.

pp. 6-7. Bahá'u'lláh, *Tablets of Bahá'u'lláh revealed after the Kitáb-i-Aqdas,* 1988, pocket-size edition, p.157

p. 8. Bahá'u'lláh, *Gleanings from the Writings of Bahá'u'lláh,* US Baha'i Publishing Trust, 1990 pocket-size edition, CXXXII: p.287

p. 9. Bahá'u'lláh, *Epistle to the Son of the Wolf,* US Baha'i Publishing Trust, 1988, p.139

pp. 10-11. Bahá'u'lláh, *Gleanings from the Writings of Bahá'u'lláh,* US Baha'i Publishing Trust, 1990 pocket-size edition, XXVII: pp.67-68

pp. 12-13. *ibid,* CLIII: pp.326-327

p. 14. *ibid,* p.326

p. 15. *ibid, CXLVII:* p.317

pp.16-17. 'Abdu'l-Bahá, *Paris Talks,* UK Bahá'í Publishing Trust, 1972, pp.127-8

p. 18. *ibid,* p.129

p. 19. *ibid,* p.53

p. 19. *ibid,* p.136

p. 20. 'Abdu'l-Bahá, *Compilation of Compilations,* Volume 2. Chapter on Trustworthiness. 1991. No. 2053

p. 21. Bahá'u'lláh, *Tablets of Bahá'u'lláh revealed after the Kitáb-i-Aqdas,* 1988, pocket-size edition, p.138

pp. 22-3. *ibid,* p.459

pp. 24-5. Story told by 'Abdu'l-Bahá, *The Diary of Juliet Thompson,* www.bahaistories.com, Truthfulness section.

pp. 26-7.	Bahá'u'lláh, *Tablets of Bahá'u'lláh revealed after the Kitáb-i-Aqdas,* 1988, pocket-size edition, p.122
p. 28.	*ibid,* p.37
p. 29.	Bahá'u'lláh, *Gleanings from the Writings of Bahá'u'lláh,* US Baha'i Publishing Trust, 1990 pocket-size edition, CXXXVI: p.297
pp. 30-1.	*ibid,* CXXXI: p.305
p. 32.	'Abdu'l-Bahá, quoted in *Bahá'u'lláh and the New Era*, J.E. Esslemont, US Bahá'í Publishing Trust, 1980. p.83
p. 33.	Bahá'u'lláh, *Gleanings from the Writings of Bahá'u'lláh,* US Baha'i Publishing Trust, 1990 pocket-size edition, CXXXII: p.289
pp. 34-5.	'Abdu'l-Bahá, *The Promulgation of Universal Peace.* US Bahá'í Publishing Trust, 1982, p.453
p.36.	*ibid.*
pp. 37.	'Abdu'l-Bahá, quoted in *Bahá'u'lláh and the New Era*, J.E. Esslemont, US Bahá'í Publishing Trust, 1980. p.83
pp. 38-39.	'Abdu'l-Bahá, *Selections from the Writings of 'Abdu'l-Bahá,* Bahá'í World Centre, 1982, p.87
p. 40.	'Abdu'l-Bahá, *Compilation of Compilations,* Volume 2. Chapter on Trustworthiness. 1991. No. 2054
p. 41.	Bahá'u'lláh, *Compilation of Compilations,* Volume 2. Chapter on Trustworthiness. 1991. No. 2050
pp. 42-3.	Bahá'u'lláh, *Tablets of Bahá'u'lláh revealed after the Kitáb-i-Aqdas,* 1988, pocket-size edition, p.40
p. 44.	'Abdu'l-Bahá, *Paris Talks,* UK Bahá'í Publishing Trust, 1972, p.118
p. 45.	Bahá'u'lláh, *The Kitáb-i-Íqán*, US Bahá'í Publishing Trust, 1989, pocket-size edition, p.43

First Published in the UK in 2014 by
Intellect, The Mill, Parnall Road, Fishponds,Bristol, BS16 3JG, UK

First published in the USA in 2014
by Intellect, The University of Chicago Press, 1427 E. 60th Street, Chicago, IL 60637, USA

A catalogue record for this book is available from the British Library.

Book Design: Corinne Randall
Publisher: Masoud Yazdani
ISBN 978-1-78320-096-2
Printed and bound by Gomer Press Ltd.

Other books in the ***Essential Insights*** series.
Healing, Mindfulness, Detachment, Openness, Oneness, Generousity, Gratefulness, Love, Simplicity, Awareness, Transformation.